WAY O.

Uniting our Sufferings to Christ

Meditations by
Rt. Rev. Michael Campbell OSA

*All booklets are published thanks to the
generous support of the members of the
Catholic Truth Society*

CATHOLIC TRUTH SOCIETY
PUBLISHERS TO THE HOLY SEE

Contents

All rights reserved. First published 2014 by The Incorporated Catholic Truth Society, 40-46 Harleyford Road London SE11 5AY Tel: 020 7640 0042 Fax: 020 7640 This edition © 2014 The Incorporated Catholic Truth Society.

Inside images: Pages 4, 6, 12, 16, 26, 28 and 32 by Josef Piens Cooreman; © Renata Sedmakova/Shutterstock.com. Pages 8, 14, 18, 22, 24 and 30 by Rene de Cramer; © Renata Sedmakova/Shutterstock.com. Page 10 by Rene de Cramer; © Renata Sedmakova. Page 20 by Josef Piens Cooreman; © Renata Sedmakova/ depositphotos.com. Page 34 © Glenda/Shutterstock.com.

ISBN 978 1 86082 898 0

Introduction

The Stations of the Cross have long been a popular and much-loved Catholic devotion. To walk the way of the cross with the suffering Christ, prayerfully contemplating his humiliation and suffering, gives us the courage to accept and bear our own particular share of the cross, whatever form that may take.

This cherished devotional practice teaches us the profound and mysterious lesson that it was through his suffering and cross that the Son of God redeemed the world. The Stations offer the sick and frail, those who are oppressed and downcast, the opportunity to unite their sufferings with those of Christ and to make their own the sentiments of St Paul, "to complete what is lacking in Christ's affliction for the sake of his body, that is, the Church." (*Col* 1:24)

I offer these meditations on the Stations of the Cross in the hope that all who use them will draw closer to our blessed Lord who loves each one of us in our weakness and frailty. Through walking the way to Calvary with Christ may we be brought to the glory of his resurrection.

✠ Michael Campbell OSA
Bishop of Lancaster

Tree of Paradise

The Church Fathers always compared the tree of Paradise with the tree of sin; the tree that bears the fruit of the knowledge of good and evil, of knowledge, with the tree of the Cross. The tree of Paradise did such great harm whereas the tree of the Cross brings us salvation and health, and pardons that harm. It is this itinerary that human history follows. It is a way that enables us to encounter Jesus Christ the Redeemer, who lays down his life for love.

Pope Francis
Homily on the Feast of the Exaltation of the Cross,
14th September 2013

First Station

Jesus is condemned to death

P. *(Kneeling)* We adore you, O Christ, and we praise you.

C. Because by your holy cross you have redeemed the world.

"Like a lamb led to the slaughter-house, like a sheep dumb before its shearers, he never opened his mouth." (*Is* 53:7)

P. Pilate passes the sentence of death on Jesus and he, the innocent lamb of God, goes to meet his death for the salvation of the world.

Reflection

Lord Jesus, you humbly submitted to your Father's will and obediently set out on the road to Calvary for our sake. Teach us the lessons of your Passion, and in the Father's will let us find our peace. Give us generosity of spirit to accept without complaint our situation in life, and the faith to believe that you are never far from any of us. For you are Emmanuel, God-with-us.

C. I love you, Jesus, my love above all things. I repent with my whole heart of having offended you. Never permit me to separate myself from you again. Grant that I may love you always and then do with me what you will.

Our Father…Hail Mary…Glory be…

Second Station

Jesus receives his cross

P. *(Kneeling)* We adore you, O Christ, and we praise you.

C. Because by your holy cross you have redeemed the world.

"And carrying his own cross he went out of the city to the place of The Skull, or, as it was called in Hebrew, Golgotha." (*Jn* **19:17**)

The cross is laid on Jesus as he, a condemned man, begins his journey to the place of execution. The cross was an instrument of shame, but embraced by Jesus it would become the tree of life.

Reflection

Lord Jesus, you invite us to come after you and take up our cross each day. May we willingly and patiently accept our cross through the trials of life, knowing that by your example and with the help of your grace, we will persevere to the end. Give us the wisdom to learn that when we lose our life for your sake, then we will, in truth, find it.

C. I love you, Jesus, my love above all things. I repent with my whole heart of having offended you. Never permit me to separate myself from you again. Grant that I may love you always and then do with me what you will.

Our Father…Hail Mary…Glory be…

Third Station

Jesus falls the first time

P. *(Kneeling)* We adore you, O Christ, and we praise you.

C. Because by your holy cross you have redeemed the world.

"Ours were the sufferings he bore, ours the sorrows he carried."
(*Is* 53:4)

Tradition tells us that Jesus fell three times as he carried his cross. Jesus was weak from his scourging and illtreatment at the hands of the Roman soldiers, and his strength gave out.

Reflection

Lord Jesus, you found the weight of the cross too much to bear, and you fell to the ground. Be close to us when the road gets too hard and our strength fails us. Keep us from self-pity and discouragement, and make us firm in hope. You are our high priest and can sympathise with us in our weaknesses. In all our trials and temptations let your grace be sufficient for us.

C. I love you, Jesus, my love above all things. I repent with my whole heart of having offended you. Never permit me to separate myself from you again. Grant that I may love you always and then do with me what you will.

Our Father…Hail Mary…Glory be…

Fourth Station

Jesus meets his mother

P. *(Kneeling)* We adore you, O Christ, and we praise you.

C. Because by your holy cross you have redeemed the world.

"Woman, behold thy Son." (*Jn* 19:24)

On this sorrowful journey the afflicted Christ meets Mary his mother. What must her thoughts have been as she witnessed her son being led to his death? The words of Simeon were coming true, 'A sword shall pierce your own soul'. *Lk* 2:35

Reflection

Lord Jesus, your mother Mary shared deeply in your sufferings. Your pain was her pain. We commend to you today all mothers who suffer for the sake of their children. May the steadfast example of your mother Mary be a comfort and support to them. You willed that your mother Mary should be our mother. Let her love ever surround us, and her prayer protect us all our days.

C. I love you, Jesus, my love above all things. I repent with my whole heart of having offended you. Never permit me to separate myself from you again. Grant that I may love you always and then do with me what you will.

Our Father...Hail Mary...Glory be...

Fifth Station

Simon of Cyrene helps Jesus to carry his cross

P. *(Kneeling)* We adore you, O Christ, and we praise you.

C. Because by your holy cross you have redeemed the world.

"They enlisted a passer-by, Simon of Cyrene, father of Alexander and Rufus, who was coming in from the country, to carry his cross." (*Mk* **15:21**)

Simon of Cyrene happened to be passing by and helped Jesus to carry his cross. Simon's good deed will be forever remembered, as he proved a friend to the Son of God when he most needed him.

Reflection

Lord Jesus, you taught us that the true test of our love for God is the love we show to one another. Like Simon, make us a true friend to all whom we meet along the road of life, especially the weak and suffering. Forgive us for the times we have passed by on the other side, and let us see your face in the faces of those around us. For when we reach out to others, we are ministering to you.

C. I love you, Jesus, my love above all things. I repent with my whole heart of having offended you. Never permit me to separate myself from you again. Grant that I may love you always and then do with me what you will.

Our Father…Hail Mary…Glory be…

Sixth Station

Veronica wipes the face of Jesus

P. *(Kneeling)* We adore you, O Christ, and we praise you.

C. Because by your holy cross you have redeemed the world.

"Without beauty, without majesty we saw him, no looks to attract our eyes; despised and rejected, a man of sorrows and familiar with suffering." (*Is* 53:2-4)

Veronica, moved with pity for the despised and suffering Christ, steps forward and wipes his face with a towel. Her act of kindness and great compassion would never be forgotten.

Reflection

Lord Jesus, in the midst of your suffering and distress you found someone to take pity on you. Veronica had the courage to reach out to you in your affliction. May we never fail to feel the sufferings of others, and seek to lighten their burden. Make us compassionate as our heavenly Father is compassionate, for he is close to the afflicted and broken-hearted.

C. I love you, Jesus, my love above all things. I repent with my whole heart of having offended you. Never permit me to separate myself from you again. Grant that I may love you always and then do with me what you will.

Our Father…Hail Mary…Glory be…

Seventh Station

Jesus falls the second time

P. *(Kneeling)* We adore you, O Christ, and we praise you.

C. Because by your holy cross you have redeemed the world.

"He himself bore our sins in his body on the tree. By his wounds you have been healed." (*1 P 2:24*)

Under the weight of the cross, and our sins, Jesus falls to the ground a second time. The road gets harder with each step, the demands of love ever greater.

Reflection

Lord Jesus, as you carried your cross to Calvary you had each one of us in mind, because your love is infinite and knows no limits. When we meet with difficulties and adversity in our own lives, let us recall your great love, and remember that you walk beside us every step of the way. Left to ourselves, we stumble and fall. But with the power of your grace, all things become possible for us.

C. I love you, Jesus, my love above all things. I repent with my whole heart of having offended you. Never permit me to separate myself from you again. Grant that I may love you always and then do with me what you will.

Our Father…Hail Mary…Glory be…

Eighth Station

The women of Jerusalem weep for Our Lord

P. *(Kneeling)* We adore you, O Christ, and we praise you.

C. Because by your holy cross you have redeemed the world.

"Large numbers of people followed him, and women too, who mourned and lamented for him. But Jesus turned to them and said, 'Daughters of Jerusalem, do not weep for me; weep rather for yourselves and for your children.'" (*Lk* 23:27-28)

Devout women from Jerusalem were distraught as they beheld Christ being led to his place of execution. Foreseeing the horrors that would befall the holy city, Jesus told them to weep for themselves and for their children.

Reflection

Lord Jesus, you did not ignore the sympathy of the women of Jerusalem but acknowledged their tears, grateful for a word of comfort as you toiled under the weight of your cross. Keep us from being too proud to receive a kind word, from appreciating the good motives of others.

C. I love you, Jesus, my love above all things. I repent with my whole heart of having offended you. Never permit me to separate myself from you again. Grant that I may love you always and then do with me what you will.

Our Father…Hail Mary…Glory be…

Ninth Station

Jesus falls the third time

P. *(Kneeling)* We adore you, O Christ, and we praise you.

C. Because by your holy cross you have redeemed the world.

"By his sufferings shall my servant justify many." (*Is* **53:11**)

Jesus' strength fails him and he falls to the ground a third time under the cross. He will rise and continue his painful journey, because for him, it is a journey of love.

Reflection

Lord Jesus, you carried your cross without complaint, and accepted your sufferings in complete submission to your Father's will. Your love for your Father enabled you to trust, to hope and to endure whatever lay ahead. Inspire us, Lord, by your example of love confidently to embrace the difficulties and challenges of our own situation with trust in God, who is our loving Father.

C. I love you, Jesus, my love above all things. I repent with my whole heart of having offended you. Never permit me to separate myself from you again. Grant that I may love you always and then do with me what you will.

Our Father...Hail Mary...Glory be...

Tenth Station

Jesus is stripped of his garments

P. *(Kneeling)* We adore you, O Christ, and we praise you.

C. Because by your holy cross you have redeemed the world.

"When the soldiers had finished crucifying Jesus they took his clothing and divided it into four parts, one for each soldier."
(Jn 19:23)

At the place of execution Christ was stripped of his dignity and publicly humiliated. The soldiers then cast lots for his clothes, adding insult to their act of shame.

Reflection

Lord Jesus, you became an object of derision for our sake. Through our holy anointing in Baptism you call us to be your witnesses in today's world. We pray that we will never be ashamed of our faith, or be afraid of scorn and ridicule for the sake of your name. May we always be prepared to give a reason for the hope that is within us. Teach us the enduring lesson of your Passion that when we are weak, it is then that we find strength.

C. I love you, Jesus, my love above all things. I repent with my whole heart of having offended you. Never permit me to separate myself from you again. Grant that I may love you always and then do with me what you will.

Our Father…Hail Mary…Glory be…

Eleventh Station

Jesus is nailed to the cross

P. *(Kneeling)* We adore you, O Christ, and we praise you.

C. Because by your holy cross you have redeemed the world.

"When they reached the place of The Skull, there they crucified him and the two criminals, one on his right, the other on his left." (*Lk* 23:33)

The last, brutal act of the soldiers now unfolds and they nail Jesus to the cross. He is placed between two criminals, and his humiliation is complete.

Reflection

Lord Jesus, you were born poor in a stable, and were crucified naked on Calvary between two thieves. Your selfabasement was now complete. The love you showed for us knew no limits, even to dying on a cross. You became poor for our sakes, so that through your poverty we might become rich. Lord, let us unite our sufferings with yours and come to make our own the wisdom of the cross. Then we shall indeed be rich, and know true peace.

C. I love you, Jesus, my love above all things. I repent with my whole heart of having offended you. Never permit me to separate myself from you again. Grant that I may love you always and then do with me what you will.

Our Father...Hail Mary...Glory be...

Twelfth Station

Jesus dies on the cross

P. *(Kneeling)* We adore you, O Christ, and we praise you.

C. Because by your holy cross you have redeemed the world.

"Jesus cried out in a loud voice saying, 'Father, into your hands I commend my spirit'. With these words he breathed his last." (*Lk* **23:46**)

At the moment of death Jesus surrenders himself into the hands of his Father. His life's work is done.

Reflection

Lord Jesus, our crucified Saviour, you embraced death so that we might not die forever. By your selfless love you transformed the wood of the cross into the tree of life, and so drew us all to yourself. Following your example, when the hour of our death comes may we too, exclaim with you 'Father, into your hands I commend my spirit.'

C. I love you, Jesus, my love above all things. I repent with my whole heart of having offended you. Never permit me to separate myself from you again. Grant that I may love you always and then do with me what you will.

Our Father...Hail Mary...Glory be...

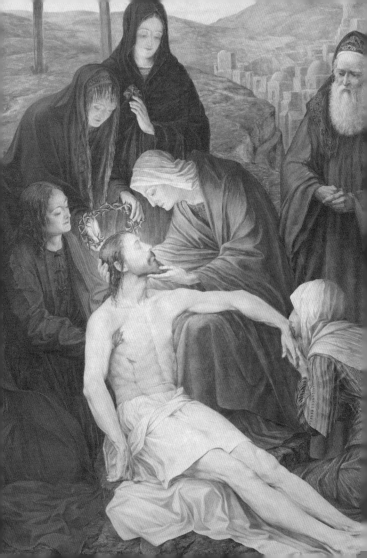

Thirteenth Station

Jesus is taken down from the cross

P. *(Kneeling)* We adore you, O Christ, and we praise you.

C. Because by your holy cross you have redeemed the world.

**"Joseph of Arimathaea went to Pilate and asked for the body
of Jesus. Then Pilate ordered it to be handed over."**
(*Mt* 27:57-58)

The lifeless body of Jesus is now taken down from the cross,
wrapped in clean linen and about to be laid in the tomb.

Reflection

Lord Jesus, by becoming a man you shared fully in all
that belongs to us. You entered the dark night of death
and would destroy its power over mankind. Death would
no longer have any power over you. In your death is our
hope, for in dying you destroyed our death and restored us
to friendship with our heavenly Father.

C. I love you, Jesus, my love above all things. I repent with
my whole heart of having offended you. Never permit me
to separate myself from you again. Grant that I may love
you always and then do with me what you will.

Our Father…Hail Mary…Glory be…

Fourteenth Station

Jesus is laid in the tomb

P. *(Kneeling)* We adore you, O Christ, and we praise you.

C. Because by your holy cross you have redeemed the world.

"At the place where he had been crucified there was a garden, and in the garden a new tomb in which no one had yet been buried. Since it was the Jewish Day of Preparation and the tomb was near at hand, they laid Jesus there." (*Jn* 19:41-42)

Joseph and Nicodemus lovingly laid the body of Jesus in a new tomb. His mother and the other women stood watching, observing the place where he was buried.

Reflection

Lord Jesus, we profess in the Creed that for our salvation, you suffered under Pontius Pilate, were crucified, died and buried. You laid down your life at a time of your own choosing, because you are the Son of the eternal Father. We do not know the day or the hour of our death, but we place all our trust in you. We pray that you will welcome us into our heavenly home, where, with the Father and the Holy Spirit, you will be all in all.

C. I love you, Jesus, my love above all things. I repent with my whole heart of having offended you. Never permit me to separate myself from you again. Grant that I may love you always and then do with me what you will.

Our Father…Hail Mary…Glory be…

Fifteenth Station

The Resurrection

P. *(Kneeling)* We adore you, O Christ, and we praise you.

C. Because by your holy cross you have redeemed the world.

**"On the first day of the week, at the first sign of dawn,
they went to the tomb with the spices they had prepared.
They found that the stone had been rolled away from the
tomb, but on entering they could not find the body
of the Lord Jesus." (*Lk* 24:1-3)**

Mary Magdalene and the other women who had stood at the
foot of the cross and watched Jesus die, now came early on
Sunday morning to perform their last religious duty for their
master, and anoint the body of the crucified Jesus. When they
reached the tomb they discovered he was no longer there.

Reflection

Lord Jesus, your death did not mark the final chapter in
the story. Death could have no power over you, nor
would your Father allow his Holy One to experience the
corruption of the tomb. In your Resurrection you rose to
a new and glorious life where tears, suffering and death
would be no more. Lord, your Resurrection is the pledge
and promise of our resurrection when our life here on earth
ends. As we complete our Way of the Cross, deepen our
faith in the resurrection of the body and the life of the
world to come.

Your victory over the power of evil and death means that we will always be an Easter people, destined to live with you, the risen Christ, for ever and ever, amen.

C. I love you, Jesus, my love above all things. I repent with my whole heart of having offended you. Never permit me to separate myself from you again. Grant that I may love you always and then do with me what you will.

Our Father…Hail Mary…Glory be…

New Companion to Lent

Taking 'personal and heartfelt conversion' as its central theme, this booklet unfolds the Lenten practices of prayer, fasting and almsgiving, particularly as part of preparing for Easter. Full of spiritual insight culled from centuries of Christian experience, and astutely balanced with practical advice for people of today, this companion also offers advice on making a retreat, a good confession, and understanding some of the key themes of the scriptures and liturgy during Lent and Holy Week.

Do740   ISBN 978 1 86082 361 9

Way of Calvary

Stations of the Cross with Benedict XVI

In these Stations of the Cross, Pope Benedict XVI reminds us that to reflect on Christ's suffering on the way of Calvary is to reflect on his love for us and his ultimate victory over death. The Holy Father's words are accompanied by beautiful images of the stunning Spanish statues used during the celebration of the Via Crucis during the last World Youth Day in Madrid.

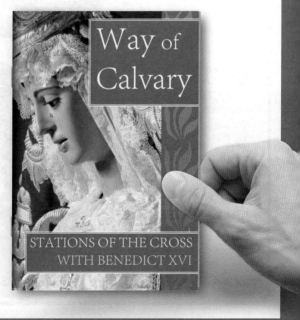

D749   ISBN 978 1 86082 782 2